WEAVING A
CALIFORNIA TRADITION

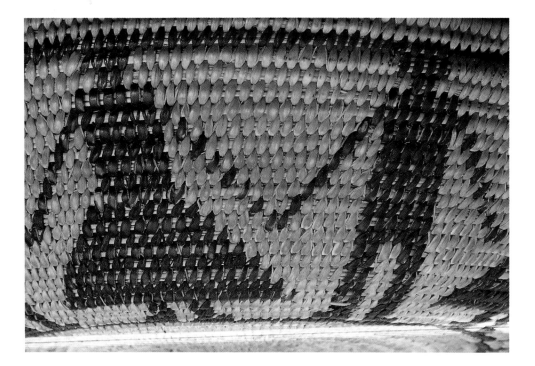

WEAVING A CALIFORNIA TRADITION

A Native American Basketmaker

Linda Yamane

Photographs by Dugan Aguilar

Lerner Publications Company ○ Minneapolis

Series Editors: LeeAnne Engfer, Gordon Regguinti
Series Consultants: W. Roger Buffalohead, Juanita G. Corbine Espinosa

Linda Yamane gives special thanks to Julie Tex and Western Mono elder Norma
Turner for sharing their culture with the readers of this book. Dugan Aguilar would
like to thank the California Indian Basketweavers Association for their help, giving
him the opportunity to photograph for this book. He also thanks his family and wife
for their continued support.

Illustrations by Linda Yamane

Lerner Publications Company
A division of Lerner Publishing Group
241 First Avenue North
Minneapolis, MN 55401 U.S.A.

Website address: www.lernerbooks.com

Library of Congress Cataloging-in-Publication Data

Yamane, Linda.
    Weaving a California tradition : a Native American basketmaker/
by Linda Yamane ; photographs by Dugan Aguilar.
       p. cm.
    Includes bibliographical references.
    Summary: Follows an eleven-year-old Western Mono Indian as she and her
relatives prepare materials needed for basketweaving, make the baskets, and attend
the California Indian Basketweavers Association's annual gathering.
    ISBN 0-8225-2660-3 (lib. bdg. : alk. paper)
    1. Mono baskets—Juvenile literature. 2. Mono Indians—Social life and customs—
Juvenile literature. 3. Basket making—California—Juvenile literature. [1. Mono
Indians. 2. Indians of North America—Juvenile literature. 3. Basket making]
I. Aguilar, Dugan, ill. II. Title.
E99.M86Y35 1997
746.41'2'089974—dc20   96–13388

Manufactured in the United States of America
3 4 5 6 7 8 – JR – 08 07 06 05 04 03

This book is dedicated to Carly and Erin Tex . . . and to hummingbird, the Western Mono healer.
—Linda Yamane

I dedicate this book to all native people from California and Nevada.
—Dugan Aguilar

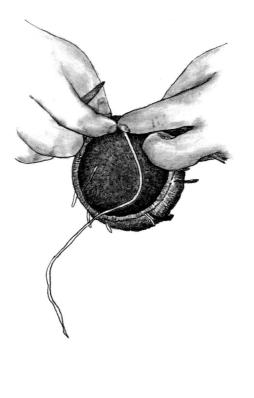

Preface

Weaving a California Indian basket cannot be done in an afternoon or a day. The process can take weeks or months—sometimes even years. In many ways, it has become difficult to continue the tradition of basketweaving. There are fewer weavers to pass on the knowledge, and people are busy working, going to school, or raising their children. It can be hard to find time for weaving in this busy, modern life.

Many of the natural places where plants grow have been turned into roads, housing developments, and shopping centers. Even in orchards and farmlands, plants that weavers have traditionally used are hard to find. When weavers do find the plants, it might not be possible to get permission from the owner of the land to gather them.

In spite of the difficulties so many basketweavers face, we have a strong determination to keep these traditions alive. It is a way of saying, "We are proud of our ancestors. We are proud of how they lived their lives. They are part of us and we are part of them, and we remember and honor them by continuing the traditions they began."

I've spent many years learning about the basketry of my Ohlone ancestors. In my area, the basket tradition was lost. There are very few Ohlone baskets left, and they are so scattered that it was quite a job to learn enough to be able to begin weaving our baskets again. When I did, it was very exciting, because these were probably the first Ohlone baskets to be made in nearly a hundred years! Making baskets is my way of bringing honor and respect to my ancestors.

In this book, you will meet Carly Tex, who is Western Mono, and her family. I hope that through their story you will learn how much time it takes to gather the plants used in basketry and prepare them for weaving. I hope you will learn that making baskets is not an easy job—it is complicated. But the job is also filled with joy, for as basketweavers, we work together. We spend time with the plants. We learn from the earth.

Linda Yamane

—*Linda Yamane*

*F*or Carly Tex and her family, basketmaking is more than just a craft or a beautiful art form. They make baskets because that is what their family has always done. Carly is 11 years old and comes from a long line of Western Mono basketweavers. Carly lives with her mom and dad and her seven-year-old sister, Erin, in Dunlap, California, a small town in the foothills of the Sierra Nevada Mountains.

Carly, her sister Erin, and their parents, Dale and Julie, live in Dunlap, California. Carly's older sister, Mandy, doesn't live at home anymore. She goes to college in Fresno.

Carly and her family are all involved in one way or another with basketmaking, but they also do many other things. Carly's mom, Julie Tex, has a college degree in anthropology and has recently returned to college to earn a graduate degree in social work. It's a lot of work going to school, studying, and taking care of her family.

Carly's older sister, Mandy Marine, also goes to college, at Fresno State University. She will graduate soon with a degree in anthropology.

Carly's dad, Dale Tex, is well known for his beadwork. He creates his own designs, using many colors. He made Carly's mom a belt with 18,000 beads in it!

The rolling countryside where Carly's family lives is home to many birds and animals. In winter, the air is crisp and cold. Some shrubs and trees shed their leaves during the cold season, but others keep theirs, so the land still looks green. By springtime, the trees have budded new leaves, plants grow lush and green, and the hills, meadows, and roadsides are filled with colorful wildflowers. During the hot summer, the land turns to yellows and browns. Seeds begin to ripen. In fall, the weather gradually cools and the oak trees begin to drop their acorns to the ground. Some trees and shrubs lose their leaves once again, and the cycle of the seasons continues.

It's hard to say just how many generations of Western Mono people have lived in this area. Some elders remember that when they were little, their elders said the Monos had once lived on the eastern side of the Sierra Nevada Mountains. Many Mono people still have relatives on the other side of the mountains. In fact, the Western Mono language is very similar to the languages spoken by the Northern Paiutes, the Bannocks, and the Northern Shoshones, Indian people who now live in Nevada, Utah, Idaho, California, Wyoming, and northern Arizona.

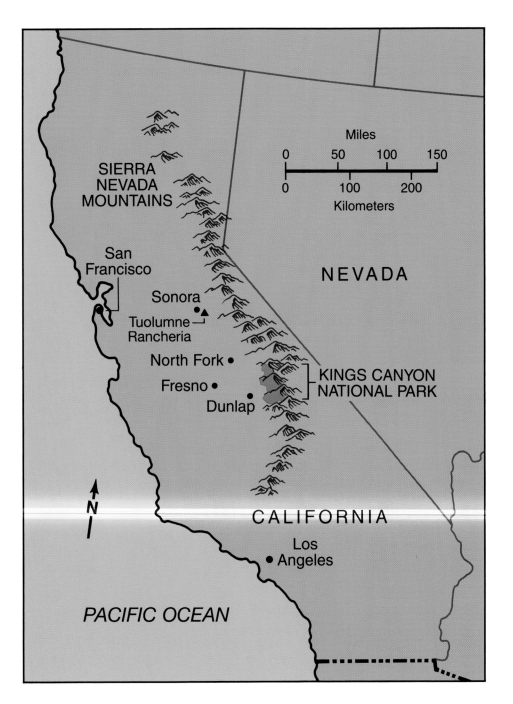

The Western Monos are one of many California Indian tribes. You may have heard of the Cahuilla, Chumash, Pomo, Yurok, or Yokuts. There are nearly 60 tribes in California, and most of them are made up of many smaller tribal groups. For example, there are several Western Mono groups. Carly's mother, Julie, is Dunlap Mono. Carly's father, Dale, is North Fork Mono.

Carly enjoys riding her bike in the countryside near her home.

Although Julie's family has lived in this area for hundreds of years, the Dunlap Band of Western Monos are not yet recognized as a tribe by the United States government. Some California Indian tribes are federally recognized, including some Western Monos. They have reservation lands, usually called *rancherias.*

Most California Indian people live typical American lives—they buy food from grocery stores, watch television, go to school, and work at many different kinds of jobs. But they also practice traditions that have been passed down for many generations and that bind them together as a community. Sometimes Indian people feel as though they live in two very different worlds, but most of the time it just feels natural to combine all of these things.

In the past, baskets were a necessary part of everyday life. Carly's ancestors cooked in baskets, ate from baskets, carried their babies in basket cradleboards, gathered seeds in baskets, sifted acorn flour on basket trays, wore basket hats, gave baskets as gifts, stored food and treasures in baskets, and used baskets in important ceremonies.

In the modern world, people don't have to use baskets every day. There are bags and boxes, plastic containers, dishes, pots and pans, and many different kinds of baby carriers. Although Indian people do not use baskets as often as in the past, they still use them in ceremonies, for preparing foods, as special gifts, and to carry babies.

*C*arly made her first basket when she was eight years old. It was a miniature cradleboard, only about six inches long. A cradleboard is a kind of cradle or carrier to hold a baby. There are many different styles of Native American cradles. Some are made of wooden frames or backboards. Many are covered with animal skins or fabric and padded for comfort.

In California, baskets serve as baby cradles. The shape and materials of cradleboards vary throughout California, but they are always made to be both sturdy and comfortable. Most have a hood at the top that protects the baby's face from the sun. The baby is wrapped in a blanket and tied securely into the cradleboard with a crisscrossing cord or sash.

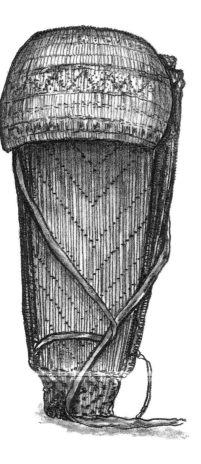

Western Mono people still use cradleboards, but not many people know how to make them. Carly's Aunt Gladys is a basketweaver, and she gets lots of requests for cradleboards. Even people from neighboring tribes ask her to make them, so Gladys is always busy weaving or preparing sticks and roots for a basket.

A Western Mono baby's first basket is called a *pusuk* (PUH-suhk). A long time ago, when a baby outgrew its *pusuk,* the basket was left hanging in a young pine tree so the child would grow fast like the growing pine. But when non-Indian people came along, they started collecting baskets, and they took them out of the trees. Because of that, Western Mono people stopped putting their baskets out, and the tradition ended. When children outgrow the *pusuk* they are moved into a larger cradleboard called a *hoop.*

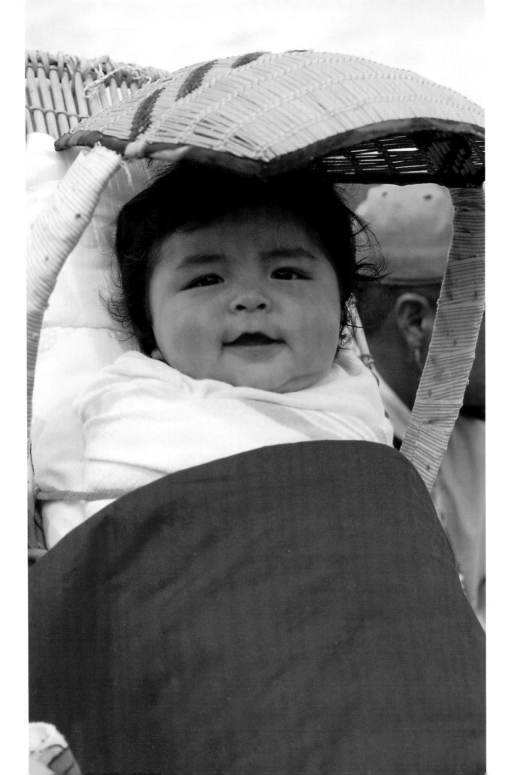

Babies feel secure in a cradleboard.

Like most children who are raised in a baby basket, Carly felt secure and safe in her cradleboard. Even when she was getting a little older, she liked to climb in it to sleep. The family laughs when they remember how Carly grew too big for her cradleboard and her feet hung over the edge.

Carly's mom, Julie, also had a cradleboard when she was a baby. That basket was made by Julie's great-aunt, Annie Charley, who was called Hoochie, which means "paternal grandmother" in the Mono language. Since Julie's grandmother had died, her great-aunt took on the responsibility of making the basket. The hood on Julie's cradleboard is closed all the way to the back. This is the Dunlap style.

Traditionally, a boy's cradleboard is woven with straight lines or a V pattern across the back, because a boy needs to shoot straight to be a good hunter. Zigzag or diamond patterns are used for girls' cradles, because these patterns suggest movement and activity. Women who are lazy might not take care of their families, so girls are encouraged to be busy, even from the time they are wrapped in their cradleboards.

The cradleboard on the left was made for Carly by her grandmother, Avis Punkin. In Western Mono culture, a baby's paternal grandmother (the father's mother) makes the cradleboard. The older cradleboard on the right was made for Carly's mother when she was a baby by her great-aunt, Annie Charley, because her grandmother had died.

17

When Carly finished her first basket, she gave it away. In Western Mono custom, a weaver gives away her first basket. This helps her learn generosity and discourages greed. Carly presented her first cradleboard to her father's mother. Carly's grandmother was so touched by the gift that she in turn gave Carly's father a basket his grandmother had made for him. Carly felt really proud. It was a special occasion for the whole family.

With guidance from her mother and her Aunt Gladys, Carly has been working on a larger cradleboard. This basket is about 18 inches long (still smaller than the size needed for a baby), and she is weaving it in a boy's design. When Carly finishes it, she'll give it to Erin, who plans to use it for her doll.

Although Carly is a basketweaver, she certainly doesn't make baskets all the time. Like most kids, she spends a lot of her time in school. One of her favorite activities is computer lab. She also loves recess. On nice days, Carly and her friends like to talk and play outside.

School days are busy. Carly's class often visits the school library, and Carly also takes flute lessons. This is her first year to study flute. Her teacher hopes she'll continue, because he thinks she can be a good flute player. She also plays the piano. Carly used to play her great-grandfather's piano, but it was destroyed in a fire. Now she practices on her electronic keyboard or on her Aunt Flo's piano.

Carly and Erin spend some time with their Aunt Flo.

In Western Mono culture, aunts are as important as mothers. Carly and her sister are lucky to have their mother's two sisters living nearby. Florence Dick, or Aunt Flo, travels throughout California as a state employee. Gladys McKinney, the other aunt, teaches about California Indian culture in schools and museums. No matter how busy Florence and Gladys are, they always find time to spend with their nieces.

21

At the powwow, Carly, Erin, and Dale eat Indian tacos and buy beads for Dale's beadwork. Dale says he's able to create beautiful beadwork patterns because of the many generations of basketweavers in his family.

Another thing Carly enjoys is going to powwows. Powwows aren't a California Indian tradition, but the whole family enjoys the atmosphere. They like to visit with friends and relatives, eat Indian tacos (tacos made on frybread), buy beads for Dale's beadwork, and watch Erin Tex dance.

Erin has fun dancing at powwows with her cousin, who is Mono, Ojibway, and Cherokee. The kind of dancing people do at powwows was not part of Western Mono culture in the past, but now it is Erin's way of participating in the larger Indian community.

Erin's older sister made the dress and shawl that Erin wears when she dances, and her mom made her moccasins. Erin's cousin taught her to dance.

When most people think about what it takes to make a basket, they just think of the weaving. But a lot of hard work must be done before the weaving can begin. First, the proper plants must be gathered. Each plant is gathered at a certain time of the year.

The geography and climate of an area determine the kinds of plants that grow there. Generally, northern California baskets are made from different plants than those used by central California weavers. Still other plants are used in southern California. Within these regions, each tribal group has its own unique style.

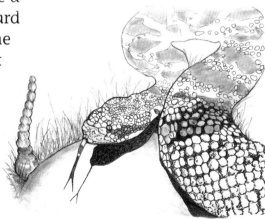

Western Mono basketweavers use deergrass, chaparral, sourberry, redbud, sedge, and bracken fern. Deergrass is a bunchgrass (a grass that grows in tufts). Deergrass has narrow flower stalks that are gathered in the fall and dried to use in baskets.

In the past, California Indian people burned fields of grasses every year. After a fire, more seeds sprout, and there are fewer insects in the area to infest plants. Deergrass needs to be burned regularly so it will be healthy and produce lots of flower stalks. When redbud is burned, it responds by growing new, long, straight shoots. These days, it's against the law for most people to set fires, so weavers have a hard time finding good basket materials.

Carly's mom and her Aunt Gladys are trying to help solve this problem by working with the United States Forest Service. The Forest Service in their area is trying to help weavers by burning plants like deergrass and redbud at regular intervals.

The part of the sedge plant that is used for baskets grows underneath the ground rather than on top. Sedge plants send out long runners, called *rhizomes,* that connect one plant with another. These runners, often called "white root" by weavers, are carefully dug out of the ground in spring. The runners are clipped at the base of each plant, then split

in half lengthwise, exposing a light-colored, woody strand inside. Each smooth strand is separated from its outer covering of bark. Then the strands are coiled together and stored to dry. The dried sedge strands are soaked in water, then carefully trimmed before being used for weaving.

Bracken fern also has an underground runner that is used in Western Mono basketry, but it is very different from the sedge runner. Inside the thick, gnarly bracken fern rhizome are stringy fibers in a wet, sticky substance. A dark brown band of material also runs the length of the rhizome. This woody band is used in baskets. Weavers sometimes call it "black root," because after soaking the material in water along with acorn shells, it turns a beautiful black color.

Chaparral, sourberry, and redbud are shrubs. Western Mono weavers use the young, straight shoots in their baskets. Usually the bark is scraped or peeled off when the cuttings are fresh. The bark is most often left on redbud, though, because of its beautiful reddish brown color. The redbud sticks are split lengthwise, then coiled and dried. Later, they are soaked in water and trimmed before weaving. Sourberry shoots are dried and used as the sturdy foundation sticks in work baskets and baby baskets. Chaparral sticks are used mostly to reinforce baskets in places where they need to be especially strong, such as around the rims.

Julie and Carly bundle redbud sticks.

In the summer, Carly and her family also gather the red berries from the sourberry plant. Sourberries can be eaten fresh or dried. They are *really* sour—worse than a dill pickle! As Carly and the others walk among the sourberry bushes, they watch out for rattlesnakes. The strong scent of the sourberry plants fills the air. Many Western Mono people say the smell reminds them of their grandmothers, who were often busy scraping sourberry sticks for their baskets.

Carly is weaving her cradleboard from redbud, sourberry, and sedge. First she had to gather the materials and prepare them. Redbud, chaparral, and sourberry shoots are cut in late fall or early winter, after the first frosts have caused the leaves to fall from the plants. It's a cold time of the year in the mountains, but it's also beautiful.

Carly and her family enjoy spending this time together outdoors. They laugh and talk and sing songs as they cut enough sticks to last throughout the year. They look for sticks of the right length and thickness for different kinds of baskets.

They find some materials close to home, but sometimes they have to travel long distances to find the plants they need. Sometimes they gather on private land. Other times they find what they're looking for on public land or along roadsides. Carly and Erin remember a time when they went to gather redbud where they always had, but someone had built a house there. The redbud was gone.

When weavers collect plants, they are careful not to take too many or to destroy them. In fact, the cutting, trimming, and thinning benefits the plants. Sedge plants with underground runners that were crowded have room to spread out and grow long and straight. Redbud and other shrubs that are cut back will have less insects and grow healthy new shoots. Weavers take care of the plants and are taught to say "thank you" to the Creator, the plants, and the earth for what they take.

After the weaving materials are gathered, they must be prepared—very soon after gathering, before they dry out. Sticks and roots usually need to be scraped or peeled to remove the bark. Sedge roots must be split lengthwise. It takes practice, patience, and a delicate touch to learn how to split roots properly. Bracken fern requires lots and lots of scraping and cleaning to remove the sticky material.

Mandy gathers redbud shoots.

29

Carly, Mandy, Gladys, and Julie have had a good time gathering basketry materials together.

After the materials have been split, scraped, or peeled, they are tied into coils or bundles for drying. Basket materials usually must dry for six months to a year before they can be used.

Preparing for weaving involves a lot of hard work, but the jobs can be fun when done in a group. Carly and her family sometimes gather and prepare materials by themselves, but other times they share the work with people who are just learning to weave. This way they can pass along traditions that might otherwise be forgotten.

*L*ast year, Carly gathered and prepared enough redbud to make a full-sized gathering basket called a *sumaya* (soo-MY-yuh). It is oval in shape and gradually becomes deeper in the center. The sumaya is not tightly woven, but has spaces between the rows of weaving. It is made entirely of redbud, except for the rim, which is chaparral.

Carly's Aunt Gladys taught her that for a sumaya, she should look for short young redbud shoots without any nubs. These were for the basket's framework. She also looked for nice long sticks to split for the weavers, which are used to weave around the foundation or frame sticks. Carly had to find a special chaparral stick to use for the rim. It had to be long enough to curve around the whole edge of her sumaya.

California Indians have two ways of constructing baskets—*coiling* and *twining.* Cradleboards and sumayas are both twined baskets. Twined baskets have a framework of sticks. The weaver attaches these sticks together by twisting pairs of flexible weaving strands around them, row after row. Gladys taught Carly how to add new sticks to her sumaya frame to make the basket broader and deeper. Carly had to use her math skills to find the right places to add new sticks evenly. She counted the number of sticks in the basket and divided that by the number of new sticks she wanted to add. Then she knew the number of sticks that she should leave between each new one she added.

In the twining technique shown here, two strands of weaving material are twisted around the foundation sticks. The stitches may be formed around every single stick, as shown, or around pairs of sticks.

Shaping the sumaya was tricky, too, but Carly enjoyed doing it. Making the cradleboard was easier, she says, but the sumaya was more challenging, because she had to be patient and use more sticks.

Carly works on her second cradleboard, twining redbud strands in a boy's V pattern.

In coiled basketry, the stitching material wraps around a single stick, a bundle of three sticks, or a bundle of grasses. Each time the strand wraps around, it is attached to the row below.

Coiling is quite different from twining. Coiled baskets start out with a tight coil of flexible plant material. This becomes the center bottom of the basket. The weaver wraps a long, narrow strand of dampened material, such as sedge or redbud, around a foundation material.

The weaving materials used in coiled baskets vary according to tribal tradition. For Western Mono baskets, the core or foundation material is a small bundle of deergrass. Weavers from other areas use willow sticks.

As each dampened strand is wrapped around the foundation, the weaver pokes a small hole into the row below it. Before the hole closes up, she pushes the strand through the hole and pulls the stitch tight.

A sharp, pointed tool called an awl is used to make the hole. Some weavers use a modern awl made of metal. Others prefer to use a traditional awl made of a sharpened piece of deer bone.

Carly has worked hard to finish her sumaya in time for this year's California Indian Basketweavers Gathering. These annual gatherings are a time when basketmakers from throughout the state come to share their weaving skills and their love of baskets. Beginners, young or old, learn from more experienced weavers. There are many different tribal groups and styles of baskets, but the weavers all share a common bond.

This year's gathering is at the Tuolumne Rancheria, near Sonora. Carly is looking forward to entering her sumaya in the Basketweavers Showcase. The showcase is a display of baskets completed by California Indian basketweavers during the previous year. The showcase encourages weavers to find the time to work on their baskets, giving them a goal to work toward. It also inspires others to learn to weave.

Most California Indian baskets take a *very* long time to make. The amount of time depends on the type of basket and the size. A basket that is very tightly woven with fine weaving materials takes longer to make than an open-weave basket or one made with heavier materials. Because many weavers are busy working, going to school, or raising families, they are lucky to finish one or two baskets a year.

Top left: *Nancy Richardson (Karuk).* Bottom left: *Western Mono weavers Ruby Pomona, Ethel Temple, Julie Tex, Carly Tex, and Norma Turner.* Below: *Martha Beecher (Western Mono).*

At this year's basket-weavers gathering, people have come from near and far. Everyone is busy and excited. Carly's whole family is here, including some cousins.

During the first day of the gathering, weavers and their families and friends spend time together away from the public eye. It is a day for teaching and learning, and Carly does some of both. She sits next to her Aunt Gladys for a while, watching as Gladys begins a coiled basket. Carly and her cousin prepare deergrass for Gladys. As they work, Erin gives some helpful advice to a beginning weaver. Later, the girls prepare sedge strands by trimming them with a knife until they are nice and thin. These long strands will be wrapped and stitched around the deergrass foundation.

Above: *Carly and her cousin Candace prepare deergrass to be used in a coiled basket.*
Right: *Carly watches Gladys weave a coiled basket.*

37

The hours pass quickly, and soon Carly hears the announcement that it is time to enter the baskets into the showcase. This is the moment she has been waiting for. She proudly shows off her sumaya to her family one last time before heading off with Erin to the check-in station. She fills out a registration form and leaves her basket there. It will be photographed, then arranged in the exhibit. The showcase won't be ready for viewing until tomorrow.

After the evening meal, as the warm night darkens, people begin getting up to share the stories and songs of their tribal areas. By bedtime, Carly and Erin are tired and ready for a good night's sleep.

Carly and others enjoy a meal in front of the traditional roundhouse at Tuolumne Rancheria.

The next morning, everyone gets up early. All the weavers help set up displays for the many visitors who will arrive soon, since the exhibit is open to the public.

All day long, Carly and the others demonstrate aspects of California Indian culture. Mandy shows how to make string from the silvery fibers found in the stem of the milkweed plant. She rolls and twists the long, soft fibers. In the old times, milkweed string was woven by hand into long sashes, which were used to tie babies into their cradleboards. Most modern-day people use store-bought yarn to weave sashes, because making string by hand takes a long time. Still, people like Mandy try to preserve the old ways.

Next Carly and Erin perform traditional California Indian songs. Their music turns out to be one of the highlights of the day. Carly knows about 45 songs. Different California Indian groups have their own songs, yet they all have a familiar sound. There are songs for many occasions—for dancing, for storytelling, for healing people who are sick, for protecting people from harm, for bringing people home who are away, for good luck, for hunting, for funerals, even for sending away the fog! In southern California, some songs last hours and hours. These songs tell creation stories about the beginning of the world.

Carly and Erin sing several songs, and Carly dedicates one special song to Mandy. When she finishes, Mandy, other family members, and a number of people in the audience have to wipe tears from their eyes.

Mandy is touched by the song that Carly sings for her.

40

Carly and Erin sing California Indian songs and use clapper sticks, a traditional instrument.

Carly and Erin also explain to visitors how to make clapper sticks, one of the instruments used in California Indian music. First, they peel the bark off a length of elderberry wood. Then they partially split it lengthwise, leaving a handle at the bottom. The soft inner pith is scooped out of the split section, and the whole instrument is sanded smooth. The split portion of the stick claps together when the player hits it against the palm of her hand. The sound of clapper sticks is a very ancient California sound.

Another instrument often used in traditional California Indian music is the deer-hoof rattle. Several deer hooves are hung with leather thongs or cords from a bone or wood handle. When shaken, the hooves clack together. Another kind of rattle is made from large moth cocoons. The cocoons are filled with tiny rocks and attached to a wooden handle.

Kimberly Stevenot (Northern Mewuk) mixes acorn flour with water before cooking it.

One of the most popular demonstrations at each year's basketweavers gathering is the cooking of acorn. Oak trees grow abundantly throughout California, and acorns, the nuts of the oak, have been an important food for most California Indian tribes for centuries. This year, Carly helps Julie and other family members as they demonstrate how to prepare and cook acorn the old way—in a basket with hot cooking stones.

Earlier in the week, the women shelled the acorns and removed the thin, papery husks from around the nuts. Next, they pounded the cleaned acorns into a flour. A special sifting basket tray was used to separate the fine particles from the coarse. In the past, California Indian people pounded acorns in stone mortars with heavy stone pestles. Acorns can either be pounded in the old way or ground in modern grinders.

When Julie and the others had prepared enough fine flour, they washed it in a special way to remove a bitter substance called tannic acid that is in acorns. The women poured water over the acorn flour again and again until the bitter taste was gone. After this, the acorn flour was ready to be mixed with water in a water-tight cooking basket.

Before they began cooking, Carly filled the cooking basket with water so it could soak for a while. Soaking the basket makes the basket fibers swell, which makes a tighter fit between stitches and ensures that water won't leak out during cooking. The soaking also protects the basket from the extreme heat of the cooking stones. Earlier in the day of the demonstration, people built a fire and placed several round cooking stones among the hot coals.

Finally, the cooking begins. One at a time, the hot cooking stones are removed from the fire with two long, sturdy poles (kind of like giant chopsticks). The cooking stones are carried from the fire and dipped briefly into a bucket or basket of clean water to remove the ashes. The stones are quickly rinsed a second time to be sure they are clean. They are then placed into the cooking basket with the acorn and water. Carly stirs each rock around and around in the acorn mixture with a special looped stirring stick until the rock begins to cool. At that time, another hot cooking stone is added to the basket in the same way. Before long, the acorn mixture begins to boil and bubble. By the time it's finished cooking, it has thickened into a mush. When it cools off, it will be ready to eat!

Carly is just learning to prepare acorn. She feels honored to stir the acorn in the demonstration this year. Little by little, she will learn the whole process. When the hot acorn has cooled, the audience gets to taste it. It is a very gentle food, without a strong flavor. Some people like it and some people don't. Acorn is very bland, and if you haven't grown up with the taste, you might not like it. But even people who don't care for the flavor of acorn enjoy watching it being cooked in the old way.

Carly has been so busy all day she hasn't had a chance to visit the Basketweavers Showcase to see her sumaya and all the other baskets on display. In the exhibit are all shapes and sizes of baskets. One is covered with beads. Another has little quail feathers around the rim. There are sifting baskets and baby baskets, bowls and flat trays. There is even a fish-trap basket.

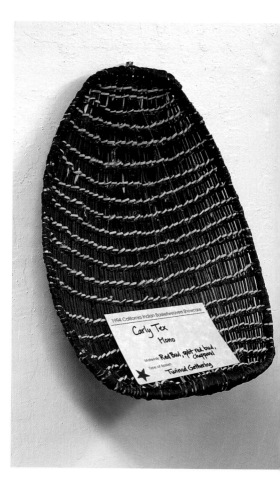

Carly is proud to see her sumaya on display with the other baskets at the Basketweavers Showcase.

Carly is proud to see her sumaya basket here among the others and wonders what kind of basket to make next year. She tells her mother she thinks she wants to make a redbud storage basket. It's a twined, deep, oval-shaped bowl. The outside will be red with a white design and the inside will be white with a red design.

Next year Carly will make her redbud storage basket. And the year after that she'll make another kind of basket . . . and the years and the baskets will go on and on. Carly likes to weave, and she wants to keep making baskets so she can carry on the tradition. "I want to keep learning and teach my own children so it can keep going through the generations," she says.

Word List

Bannock—Indian people from the western part of the United States, particularly Utah and Nevada

bunchgrass—grass that grows in tufts, found especially in the western part of the United States

clapper sticks—a traditional musical instrument used by California Indians, with two ends that clap together to make a distinctive sound

coiling—a technique for making baskets in which plant fibers are wrapped around a foundation material, coiling outward from the center as the basket is formed

cradleboard—a cradle or carrier to hold a baby. Western Mono cradleboards are woven baskets.

hoop—a Western Mono baby's second cradleboard, larger than the *pusuk*

mortar—a strong bowl or container in which material is pounded with a pestle

Ohlone (OH-loh-nee)—an Indian tribe from the West Coast of California

Paiute—Indian people from Nevada, Utah, and Colorado

pestle—a club-shaped device for pounding material in a mortar

pusuk (PUH-suhk)—the first basket, or cradle, for a Western Mono baby

rancheria—Indian reservations in California

reservation—an area of land that Indian people kept through agreement with the United States government

rhizome—a long plant stem that grows underground. *See also* runner

runner—part of a plant that grows out from the original plant to produce more plants

Shoshone (shuh-SHOW-nee)—Indian people from Utah and Nevada

sumaya (soo-MY-yuh)—a Western Mono gathering basket

tannic acid—a bitter substance in acorns and other plants

twining—a technique for making baskets in which plant fibers or shoots are interwoven onto a framework of sticks

weaver—the strands or shoots used to weave around a framework of sticks

Western Mono (MOH-noh)—an Indian tribe from central California

For Further Reading

Bean, Lowell John, and Lisa J. Bourgeault. *The Cahuilla.* Indians of North America, ed. Frank W. Porter III. New York: Chelsea House, 1989.

Gibson, Robert O. *The Chumash.* Indians of North America, ed. Frank W. Porter III. New York: Chelsea House, 1991.

Keator, Glenn, and Linda Yamane. *In Full View: Three Ways of Seeing California Plants.* Berkeley, Calif.: Heyday Books, 1995.

Margolin, Malcolm, and Yolanda Montijo, eds. *Native Ways: California Indian Stories and Memories.* Berkeley, Calif.: Heyday Books, 1995.

Newman, Sandra Corrie. *Indian Basket Weaving: How to Weave Pomo, Yurok, Pima and Navajo Baskets.* Flagstaff, Ariz.: Northland Publications, 1974.

Ortiz, Bev. *It Will Live Forever: Traditional Yosemite Indian Acorn Preparation.* Berkeley, Calif.: Heyday Books, 1991.

Swentzell, Rina. *Children of Clay: A Family of Pueblo Potters.* Minneapolis: Lerner Publications, 1992.

Temko, Florence. *Traditional Crafts from Native North America.* Minneapolis: Lerner Publications, 1996.

The Way We Lived: California Indian Reminiscences, Stories and Songs. Edited with commentary by Malcolm Margolin. Berkeley, Calif.: Heyday Books, 1993.